THE
BIBLIO DIET
COOKBOOK

Faith-Inspired Whole-Food Recipes to Boost Energy, Support Longevity, and Fight Inflammation through God's Healing Design

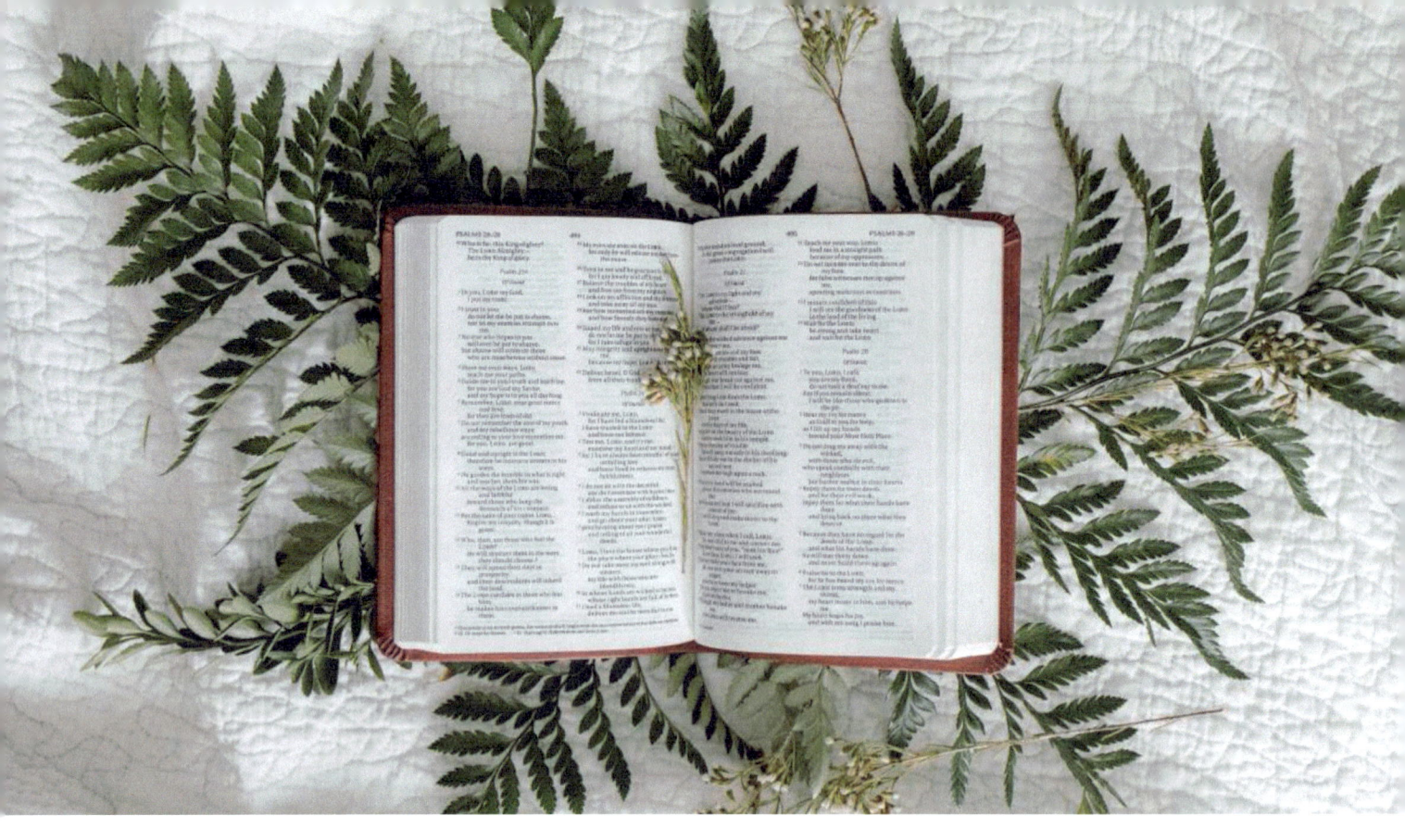

© **Copyright 2025 – Maria Heavens. All rights reserved.**

Published by Kwon Royalty Publishing, under its Tasty Shelf imprint.

The content contained within this book may not be reproduced, duplicated, or transmitted without direct written permission from the author or the publisher. Under no circumstances will any blame or legal responsibility be held against the publisher or author for any damages, reparation, or monetary loss due to the information contained within this book, either directly or indirectly.

Legal Notice:

This book is copyright protected. It is only for personal use. You may not amend, distribute, sell, use, quote, or paraphrase any part of the content within this book without the consent of the author or publisher.

Disclaimer Notice:

Please note that the information contained within this document is for educational and entertainment purposes only. All efforts have been made to present accurate, reliable, and up-to-date information. No warranties of any kind are expressed or implied. This book is not affiliated with, authorized, or endorsed by Maria Heavens. The recipes and meal plans are inspired by biblical dietary principles and designed to support health, wellness, and spiritual living. Please consult a licensed medical professional before making any changes to your diet or lifestyle. By reading this book, the reader agrees that under no circumstances is the author or publisher responsible for any losses, direct or indirect, that may occur as a result of using the information contained within this document, including but not limited to omissions, errors, or inaccuracies.

All recipes in this cookbook were tested and refined by chefs and nutrition enthusiasts to ensure practical use, flavor balance, and real-world results.

GET YOUR FREE EXCLUSIVE BONUSES NOW!

Download for Free – Simply Scan the QR Code Below!

BONUS 1 — 30-Day Meal Plan

BONUS 2 — Weekly Shopping Lists

BONUS 3 — Mediterranean Diet Recipe E-Book

SCAN HERE

Visit www.TheTastyShelf.com for More Free Recipes & Resources!

TABLE OF CONTENTS

Introduction...1
What Is the Biblio Diet?...1
My Journey with the Biblio Diet..2
The Role of Fasting in the Biblio Diet...3

Breakfast Recipes

Honey & Fig Yogurt Bowl..7
Barley Porridge with Dates & Almond Milk..8
Olive Oil & Herb Flatbread with Roasted Vegetables..9
Lentil & Egg Scramble with Za'atar...10
Roasted Sweet Potato Hash with Red Onions & Thyme...11
Shepherd's Breakfast Bowl with Chickpeas & Cucumber Yogurt.............................12
Apple & Raisin Millet Porridge with Cinnamon..13
Baked Pears with Walnuts & Raw Honey...14
Goat Cheese & Tomato Omelet with Herbs..15
Ezekiel Bread Toast with Olive Tapenade & Boiled Egg..16
Carrot-Date Muffins with Almond Flour..17
Grape & Quinoa Breakfast Salad with Mint & Olive Oil..18
Mashed Fava Beans with Olive Oil & Flatbread..19
Date & Almond Energy Bites with Ground Flax...20
Chickpea & Avocado Mash on Toasted Grain Bread...21

Lunch Recipes

Grilled Fish with Lemon, Garlic & Herbs...23
Cucumber & Chickpea Salad with Olive Oil & Dill...24
Lentil & Carrot Soup with Cumin..25
Quinoa Tabouli with Parsley, Tomato & Mint...26
Chickpea & Spinach Skillet with Olive Oil & Garlic...27
Roasted Beet Salad with Goat Cheese & Pomegranate...28
Barley & Fava Bean Stew with Leeks & Herbs..29
Stuffed Bell Peppers with Lentils, Brown Rice & Tomato..30
Spiced Lentil Wraps with Cucumber Yogurt Sauce...31
Herb-Grilled Chicken Thighs with Lemon-Tahini Sauce..32
Flatbread Wraps with Hummus, Cucumber & Greens..33
Baked Eggplant with Tomato, Onion & Olive Oil...34
Cauliflower Rice Bowl with Olives, Capers & Chickpeas..35
Zucchini Fritters with Herb Yogurt Dip..36
Sardine Salad with Arugula, Lemon & Capers..37

Dinner Recipes

Roasted Lamb with Rosemary & Pomegranate Glaze..39
Olive Oil-Baked Eggplant with Tomato & Basil...40
Vegetable Stew with Lentils & Barley..41
Baked Salmon with Herbs & Citrus..42
Mediterranean Lentil Shepherd's Pie...43
Herbed Chicken & Olive Skillet with Dates..44
Red Lentil Curry with Spinach & Garlic..45
Stuffed Grape Leaves with Quinoa & Herbs..46
Roasted Root Vegetables with Thyme & Garlic Oil..47
Spaghetti Squash with Tomato-Basil Sauce..48
Cod with Olive Tapenade & Sautéed Greens..49
Wild Rice & Roasted Carrot Pilaf..50
Vegetable & Chickpea Tagine with Apricots...51
Cauliflower & Olive Gratin (No Cheese)...52
Grilled Eggplant & Tomato Stacks with Garlic Oil..53

Drinks & Healing Tonics

Pomegranate & Honey Tonic..55
Lemon & Olive Oil Detox Drink..56
Cinnamon & Clove Herbal Tea..57
Fig & Date Smoothie...58
Cinnamon & Clove Herbal Tea..59
Fig & Date Smoothie...60
Warm Apple Cider Vinegar Tonic...61
Carrot & Orange Juice with Ginger...62
Watermelon & Basil Hydration Juice...63
Dates & Almond Milk Spiced Latte (Caffeine-Free)...64
Conclusion...65
30 Days Meal Plan...66
4 Weeks Shopping List...70
Index..74

INTRODUCTION

What Is the Biblio Diet?

The Biblio Diet is not just a way of eating. It is a return to what was always true. Rooted in ancient biblical wisdom and supported by modern nutritional science, the Biblio Diet encourages you to nourish your body with whole, God-created foods while embracing rhythms of rest, fasting, gratitude, and faith.

In Scripture, food is never just fuel. It is a blessing, a ritual, a source of healing, and a symbol of life. From the figs and honey of the Old Testament to the fish and olive oil meals shared by Jesus, the Bible offers timeless guidance on how to eat in alignment with creation, not in opposition to it.

The Biblio Diet draws from these biblical patterns to help you:

- Eat simply with natural, whole foods free from excess processing
- Support metabolism and healing with anti-inflammatory meals
- Incorporate fasting as a physical and spiritual reset
- Live mindfully and prayerfully, with gratitude as your daily practice.

This approach is not about counting every calorie or restricting entire food groups. It is about returning to balance. The meals in this cookbook are designed to reflect biblical ingredients and principles while working with your modern lifestyle. Whether you are cooking for your family, supporting a healing journey, or simply craving structure grounded in faith, this book offers practical, flavorful recipes that nourish both body and spirit.

If you have ever felt overwhelmed by fad diets, over-processed food, or inconsistent energy, the Biblio Diet offers a reset rooted in divine design. It is a lifestyle that promotes natural healing, vibrant energy, and spiritual clarity, one meal at a time.

My Journey with the Biblio Diet:

I didn't start the Biblio Diet because I wanted another trendy plan or short-term fix. I started it because I was tired. Tired of waking up with no energy, eating meals that left me more bloated than nourished, and following advice that felt disconnected from my values. I wanted a way of eating that supported my health while aligning with my faith.

That search led me to the Bible. What I found there wasn't a strict rulebook or a rigid list of dos and don'ts. Instead, I found rhythm. I saw how meals were shared slowly, prepared with intention, and centered around foods grown from the earth. Figs, grapes, olive oil, fish, grains, herbs, and honey were part of daily life. Fasting was used for healing and clarity. Prayer came before provision. And meals weren't just eaten, they were received with gratitude.

As I began to follow these patterns, my relationship with food changed. I started practicing intermittent fasting a few days a week, keeping meals simple and rooted in whole foods. I swapped processed snacks for fruit, herbs, and nourishing soups. I slowed down during meals. I prayed before eating. I kept the Sabbath and honored rest.

The result wasn't just physical. Yes, I lost weight and felt more energized. But I also found peace. I began to trust my body again. I felt more spiritually connected and less consumed by the pressure to eat perfectly.

The Biblio Diet helped me re-center. It reminded me that God's design is not restrictive. It is restorative. Healing is not only about what's on your plate, but also about what's on your heart.

This cookbook is my offering to you. It is a collection of meals that reflect biblical simplicity, flavor, and purpose. I hope it helps you find your own rhythm, your own healing, and your own joy in feeding both body and soul.

"So whether you eat or drink or whatever you do, do it all for the glory of God."
— *1 Corinthians 10:31 (NIV)*

The Role of Fasting in the Biblio Diet:

Fasting is one of the most powerful yet often overlooked health tools in both Scripture and science. In the Bible, fasting is not just a dietary discipline. It is a sacred practice used for spiritual clarity, healing, humility, and renewal. From Moses and David to Esther and Jesus, fasting was used to draw closer to God, realign the heart, and strengthen the body and spirit.

The Biblio Diet embraces fasting as a foundational part of both physical health and spiritual rhythm. You are not fasting to restrict or punish yourself. You are fasting to reset, to reconnect, and to give your body the rest it needs to heal and function the way it was designed.

Fasting in the Bible:

- Jesus fasted for 40 days in the wilderness to prepare for his ministry **(Matthew 4:2)**
- Daniel fasted from rich and indulgent foods during his time of spiritual seeking **(Daniel 10:3)**

- Esther called a national fast before taking bold action to protect her people **(Esther 4:16)**
- David fasted in times of grief, repentance, and worship **(Psalm 35:13)**

In each case, fasting brought clarity, strength, and healing. It was a spiritual discipline that also supported emotional and physical restoration.

Health Benefits of Fasting:

Modern science confirms what Scripture modeled thousands of years ago. Periods of fasting can:

- Improve insulin sensitivity and support balanced blood sugar
- Reduce inflammation and support digestion
- Stimulate cellular repair and detoxification
- Enhance mental clarity and focus
- Support fat loss without damaging metabolism

Fasting allows your body to shift from constant digestion to healing and restoration. It is a reset button built into your biology.

Practical Fasting Approaches:

Fasting does not need to be extreme to be effective. The Biblio Diet supports flexible and sustainable fasting patterns that align with your lifestyle and energy levels.

Recommended Fasting Styles:

- 12:12 (12 hours of eating, 12 hours of fasting): Gentle and ideal for beginners.
- 14:10 (14 hours fasting, 10 hours eating): Supports fat metabolism and hormonal balance.

- Spiritual fasting days: Occasional full-day or partial fasts focused on prayer, reflection, and worship.

During fasting windows, stay hydrated, drink herbal teas, and focus on prayer or journaling. When you break your fast, choose meals rich in biblical ingredients that are simple, wholesome, and satisfying.

A Mindset of Gratitude:

Fasting is not about deprivation. It is about devotion. Whether you are fasting for metabolic health or spiritual connection, let it be an act of alignment. Use this time to rest, reflect, and return to the rhythms that God designed for your well-being.

CHAPTER 1: BREAKFAST RECIPES

BREAKFAST

HONEY & FIG YOGURT BOWL

PREP TIME: 10 MINS | **COOK TIME:** 0 MINS | **SERVING:** 1

INGREDIENTS

- ½ cup plain unsweetened yogurt (goat milk or almond-based)
- 1 fresh fig, sliced
- ½ banana, sliced
- ¼ cup fresh berries (e.g. raspberries or blueberries)
- 1 tbsp raw honey
- 1 tbsp chopped walnuts
- ½ tbsp ground flaxseed
- Pinch of cinnamon

INSTRUCTIONS

- Spoon yogurt into a serving bowl.
- Top with fig slices, banana, and berries.
- Drizzle with raw honey.
- Sprinkle walnuts, flaxseed, and cinnamon over the top.
- Serve immediately and enjoy with gratitude.

STORAGE & REHEATING NOTES:

- **Refrigeration:** Best consumed fresh. Can be refrigerated (covered) for up to 24 hours.
- **Freezing:** Not recommended.
- **Reheating:** Not applicable.

Calories	Carbs	Protein	Fat	Fiber	Sodium	Cholesterol	Sugar
320kcal	36g	9g	12g	5g	50mg	5mg	18g

BREAKFAST

BARLEY PORRIDGE WITH DATES & ALMOND MILK

PREP TIME: 5 MINS
COOK TIME: 25 MINS
SERVING: 2

INGREDIENTS

- ½ cup pearled barley
- 1½ cups unsweetened almond milk
- ¼ tsp cinnamon
- ¼ tsp ground cardamom
- 3 Medjool dates, chopped
- 1 tbsp chopped almonds
- 1 tsp raw honey (optional)
- Pinch of sea salt

INSTRUCTIONS

- Rinse barley under cold water.
- In a saucepan, combine barley, almond milk, cinnamon, cardamom, and salt. Bring to a boil.
- Reduce heat, cover, and simmer for 20–25 minutes or until tender. Stir occasionally.
- Stir in chopped dates during the last 5 minutes of cooking.
- Top with almonds and drizzle with raw honey if desired. Serve warm.

STORAGE & REHEATING NOTES:

- **Refrigeration:** Store in an airtight container for up to 3 days.
- **Freezing:** Freeze in individual portions for up to 2 months.
- **Reheating:** Add a splash of almond milk and reheat on the stove or microwave until warm.

Calories	Carbs	Protein	Fat	Fiber	Sodium	Cholesterol	Sugar
280kcal	42g	6g	6g	5g	90mg	0mg	14g

BREAKFAST

OLIVE OIL & HERB FLATBREAD WITH ROASTED VEGETABLES

PREP TIME: 15 MINS
COOK TIME: 20 MINS
SERVING: 2

INGREDIENTS

For the Flatbread:
- 1 cup whole wheat flour
- 2 tbsp olive oil
- ¼ cup warm water
- ¼ tsp sea salt
- ½ tsp dried oregano

For the Topping:
- ½ zucchini, thinly sliced
- ½ red bell pepper, thinly sliced
- ½ red onion, thinly sliced
- 1 tbsp olive oil
- Pinch of salt and black pepper

INSTRUCTIONS

- Preheat oven to 400°F (200°C).
- Mix flatbread ingredients into a dough. Knead for 3–5 minutes and let rest for 10 minutes.
- Roll out into a flat round or oval shape.
- Toss vegetables with olive oil, salt, and pepper.
- Top the dough with vegetables and bake for 18–20 minutes or until golden.
- Slice and serve warm.

STORAGE & REHEATING NOTES:

- **Refrigeration:** Store cooked flatbread in the fridge for up to 3 days.
- **Freezing:** Freeze baked flatbread up to 1 month.
- **Reheating:** Reheat in a toaster oven or skillet until warm and crisp.

Calories	Carbs	Protein	Fat	Fiber	Sodium	Cholesterol	Sugar
330kcal	36g	7g	15g	4g	140mg	0mg	4g

BREAKFAST

LENTIL & EGG SCRAMBLE WITH ZA'ATAR

PREP TIME: 10 MINS
COOK TIME: 10 MINS
SERVING: 2

INGREDIENTS

- ½ cup cooked green or brown lentils
- 3 large eggs
- 1 tbsp olive oil
- ¼ tsp sea salt
- ¼ tsp ground black pepper
- ½ tsp za'atar seasoning
- ¼ cup chopped fresh parsley
- Optional: chopped cherry tomatoes or scallions for garnish

INSTRUCTIONS

- In a skillet, heat olive oil over medium heat.
- Add lentils and stir for 1–2 minutes until warmed.
- In a bowl, whisk eggs with salt, pepper, and za'atar.
- Pour eggs into skillet and cook, stirring gently, until eggs are just set.
- Remove from heat, top with parsley and optional garnishes. Serve warm.

STORAGE & REHEATING NOTES:

- **Refrigeration:** Store leftovers in an airtight container for up to 2 days.
- **Freezing:** Not recommended.
- **Reheating:** Reheat gently in a skillet over low heat until warmed through.

Calories	Carbs	Protein	Fat	Fiber	Sodium	Cholesterol	Sugar
280kcal	13g	17g	16g	4g	220mg	195mg	2g

BREAKFAST

ROASTED SWEET POTATO HASH WITH RED ONIONS & THYME

PREP TIME: 10 MINS
COOK TIME: 30 MINS
SERVING: 2

INGREDIENTS

- 1 medium sweet potato, peeled and diced
- ½ red onion, sliced
- 1 tbsp olive oil
- ¼ tsp sea salt
- ¼ tsp ground black pepper
- ½ tsp dried thyme
- Optional: chopped fresh parsley for garnish

INSTRUCTIONS

- Preheat oven to 400°F (200°C).
- On a baking sheet, toss sweet potato and onion with olive oil, salt, pepper, and thyme.
- Spread evenly and roast for 25–30 minutes, flipping halfway through, until golden and tender.
- Garnish with fresh parsley if desired and serve hot.

STORAGE & REHEATING NOTES:

- **Refrigeration:** Store in an airtight container for up to 3 days.
- **Freezing:** Freeze in a meal prep container for up to 1 month.
- **Reheating:** Reheat in the oven or skillet for best texture; microwave also works.

Calories	Carbs	Protein	Fat	Fiber	Sodium	Cholesterol	Sugar
220kcal	28g	2g	10g	5g	180mg	0mg	7g

BREAKFAST

SHEPHERD'S BREAKFAST BOWL WITH CHICKPEAS & CUCUMBER YOGURT

PREP TIME: 15 MINS
COOK TIME: 10 MINS
SERVING: 2

INGREDIENTS

For the bowl:
- 1 cup canned chickpeas, rinsed and drained
- 1 tbsp olive oil
- ¼ tsp sea salt
- ½ tsp paprika
- ¼ tsp ground cumin
- 1 small cucumber, diced
- 1 small tomato, diced
- 2 tbsp chopped parsley

For the yogurt sauce:
- ½ cup plain unsweetened yogurt (goat milk or almond-based)
- ½ small garlic clove, minced
- 1 tsp lemon juice
- Pinch of salt

INSTRUCTIONS

- Heat olive oil in a skillet over medium heat. Add chickpeas, salt, paprika, and cumin. Cook for 5–7 minutes until lightly browned.
- While chickpeas cook, stir together yogurt, garlic, lemon juice, and salt in a small bowl.
- In serving bowls, layer warm chickpeas with diced cucumber, tomato, and parsley.
- Drizzle with yogurt sauce and serve immediately.

STORAGE & REHEATING NOTES:

- **Refrigeration:** Store chickpea mixture and yogurt separately for up to 3 days.
- **Freezing:** Chickpeas only (not yogurt) can be frozen up to 1 month.
- **Reheating:** Reheat chickpeas in a skillet over medium heat before serving.

Calories	Carbs	Protein	Fat	Fiber	Sodium	Cholesterol	Sugar
290kcal	24g	10g	14g	6g	220mg	5mg	5g

BREAKFAST

APPLE & RAISIN MILLET PORRIDGE WITH CINNAMON

PREP TIME: 5 MINS
COOK TIME: 25 MINS
SERVING: 2

INGREDIENTS

- ½ cup millet
- 1½ cups water
- ½ cup unsweetened almond milk
- ½ apple, diced
- 2 tbsp raisins
- ½ tsp ground cinnamon
- ½ tbsp raw honey (optional)
- Pinch of sea salt

INSTRUCTIONS

- Rinse millet thoroughly. In a saucepan, combine millet, water, and salt. Bring to a boil.
- Reduce heat, cover, and simmer for 15 minutes.
- Add almond milk, apple, raisins, and cinnamon. Simmer another 10 minutes, stirring occasionally.
- Drizzle with raw honey before serving, if desired.

STORAGE & REHEATING NOTES:

- **Refrigeration:** Store in an airtight container for up to 3 days.
- **Freezing:** Freeze in individual portions up to 1 month.
- **Reheating:** Reheat with a splash of almond milk in microwave or on stovetop.

Calories	Carbs	Protein	Fat	Fiber	Sodium	Cholesterol	Sugar
260kcal	39g	6g	6g	4g	60mg	0mg	12g

BREAKFAST

BAKED PEARS WITH WALNUTS & RAW HONEY

PREP TIME: 5 MINS
COOK TIME: 25 MINS
SERVING: 2

INGREDIENTS

- 2 ripe pears, halved and cored
- 1 tbsp olive oil
- 2 tbsp chopped walnuts
- 1 tbsp raw honey
- ½ tsp ground cinnamon
- Pinch of sea salt

INSTRUCTIONS

- Preheat oven to 375°F (190°C).
- Place pear halves cut-side up in a baking dish. Brush with olive oil.
- Sprinkle with cinnamon and sea salt. Fill centers with walnuts.
- Bake for 25 minutes or until soft and golden.
- Drizzle with raw honey before serving.

STORAGE & REHEATING NOTES:

- **Refrigeration:** Store in a sealed container for up to 3 days.
- **Freezing:** Not recommended.
- **Reheating:** Warm in oven or microwave before serving.

Calories	Carbs	Protein	Fat	Fiber	Sodium	Cholesterol	Sugar
220kcal	29g	21g	11g	4g	20mg	0mg	21g

BREAKFAST

GOAT CHEESE & TOMATO OMELET WITH HERBS

PREP TIME: 5 MINS
COOK TIME: 10 MINS
SERVING: 1

INGREDIENTS

- 2 large eggs
- 1 tbsp olive oil
- 2 tbsp soft goat cheese
- ¼ cup cherry tomatoes, halved
- 1 tbsp chopped parsley or basil
- ¼ tsp sea salt
- ⅛ tsp black pepper

INSTRUCTIONS

- In a bowl, whisk eggs with salt and pepper.
- Heat olive oil in a skillet over medium heat. Add tomatoes and cook for 2 minutes.
- Pour eggs into the skillet. Let cook undisturbed for 1–2 minutes.
- Add goat cheese and herbs to one side. Fold omelet over and cook another 1–2 minutes until just set.
- Slide onto a plate and serve hot.

STORAGE & REHEATING NOTES:

- **Refrigeration:** Store in an airtight container for up to 2 days.
- **Freezing:** Not recommended.
- **Reheating:** Gently reheat in a skillet or microwave for 30 seconds.

Calories	Carbs	Protein	Fat	Fiber	Sodium	Cholesterol	Sugar
260kcal	4g	15g	20g	1g	250mg	370mg	2g

BREAKFAST

EZEKIEL BREAD TOAST WITH OLIVE TAPENADE & BOILED EGG

PREP TIME: 10 MINS   **COOK TIME:** 10 MINS   **SERVING:** 1

INGREDIENTS

- 1 slice sprouted Ezekiel bread
- 1 hard-boiled egg, sliced
- 1½ tbsp olive tapenade
- 1 tsp extra virgin olive oil
- Optional: sprinkle of chopped parsley or cracked black pepper

INSTRUCTIONS

- Toast the Ezekiel bread slice to your liking.
- Spread olive tapenade evenly over the toast.
- Top with sliced egg and drizzle with olive oil.
- Garnish with parsley or pepper if desired. Serve immediately.

STORAGE & REHEATING NOTES:

- **Refrigeration:** Assemble fresh; store hard-boiled eggs separately for up to 4 days.
- **Freezing:** Not recommended.
- **Reheating:** Toast fresh before serving; do not microwave tapenade.

Calories	Carbs	Protein	Fat	Fiber	Sodium	Cholesterol	Sugar
240kcal	18g	10g	14g	3g	340mg	185mg	1g

BREAKFAST

CARROT-DATE MUFFINS WITH ALMOND FLOUR

PREP TIME: 10 MINS **COOK TIME:** 25 MINS **SERVING:** 6

INGREDIENTS

- 1½ cups almond flour
- 2 eggs
- ½ cup shredded carrot
- 4 Medjool dates, chopped
- ¼ tsp baking soda
- ¼ tsp sea salt
- ½ tsp cinnamon
- 2 tbsp olive oil
- 1 tsp apple cider vinegar
- Optional: 1 tbsp chopped walnuts

INSTRUCTIONS

- Preheat oven to 350ºF (175ºC). Line or grease a muffin tin.
- In a bowl, whisk eggs, olive oil, and vinegar. Stir in carrots and chopped dates.
- Add almond flour, baking soda, salt, and cinnamon. Mix until just combined.
- Spoon into muffin tin and bake for 22–25 minutes or until golden and firm to the touch.
- Let cool before serving. Add walnuts on top if desired.

STORAGE & REHEATING NOTES:

- **Refrigeration:** Store in a sealed container for up to 4 days.
- **Freezing:** Freeze up to 2 months.
- **Reheating:** Microwave 20 seconds or warm in oven at 300ºF for 5–7 minutes.

Calories	Carbs	Protein	Fat	Fiber	Sodium	Cholesterol	Sugar
210kcal	14g	6g	15g	3g	140mg	55mg	8g

BREAKFAST

GRAPE & QUINOA BREAKFAST SALAD WITH MINT & OLIVE OIL

PREP TIME: 10 MINS
COOK TIME: 15 MINS
SERVING: 2

INGREDIENTS

- ½ cup dry quinoa, rinsed
- 1 cup water
- ½ cup red or green grapes, halved
- 1 tbsp extra virgin olive oil
- 1 tbsp chopped fresh mint
- 1 tbsp chopped walnuts
- 1 tsp raw honey (optional)
- Pinch of sea salt

INSTRUCTIONS

- In a small pot, combine quinoa and water. Bring to a boil.
- Reduce heat, cover, and simmer for 12–15 minutes or until quinoa is fluffy. Let cool.
- In a bowl, toss cooked quinoa with grapes, olive oil, mint, and walnuts.
- Drizzle with raw honey and sprinkle sea salt. Serve chilled or room temp.

STORAGE & REHEATING NOTES:

- **Refrigeration:** Store in an airtight container for up to 3 days.
- **Freezing:** Not recommended.
- **Reheating:** Best served cold or at room temperature.

Calories	Carbs	Protein	Fat	Fiber	Sodium	Cholesterol	Sugar
250kcal	28g	6g	11g	4g	60mg	0mg	9g

BREAKFAST

MASHED FAVA BEANS WITH OLIVE OIL & FLATBREAD

PREP TIME: 10 MINS
COOK TIME: 15 MINS
SERVING: 2

INGREDIENTS

- 1 cup cooked fava beans (or canned, rinsed)
- 1 tbsp olive oil (plus more for garnish)
- 1 small garlic clove, minced
- ½ tsp ground cumin
- Juice of ½ lemon
- Pinch of sea salt and black pepper
- 2 small pieces whole wheat flatbread (optional for serving)

INSTRUCTIONS

- In a small saucepan, warm fava beans over medium heat with garlic and olive oil.
- Mash with a fork or potato masher until mostly smooth.
- Stir in cumin, lemon juice, salt, and pepper.
- Drizzle with more olive oil before serving. Serve warm with flatbread if desired.

STORAGE & REHEATING NOTES:

- **Refrigeration:** Store in a sealed container up to 3 days.
- **Freezing:** Freeze in small containers for up to 1 month.
- **Reheating:** Reheat gently on stove with a splash of water or oil.

Calories	Carbs	Protein	Fat	Fiber	Sodium	Cholesterol	Sugar
270kcal	25g	10g	13g	6g	190mg	0mg	2g

BREAKFAST

DATE & ALMOND ENERGY BITES WITH GROUND FLAX

PREP TIME: 10 MINS **COOK TIME:** 0 MINS **SERVING:** 6

INGREDIENTS

- ½ cup Medjool dates, pitted
- ¼ cup raw almonds
- 2 tbsp ground flaxseed
- 1 tbsp olive oil
- ¼ tsp cinnamon
- Pinch of sea salt
- Optional: 1 tsp raw honey or splash of lemon juice

INSTRUCTIONS

- In a food processor, pulse almonds until coarsely ground.
- Add dates, flaxseed, cinnamon, salt, and olive oil. Blend until mixture is sticky and forms a rough dough.
- Scoop out and roll into small balls (about 1-inch each).
- Chill for 15 minutes to set, or store in the fridge for grab-and-go snacks.

STORAGE & REHEATING NOTES:

- **Refrigeration:** Store in an airtight container for up to 1 week.
- **Freezing:** Freeze up to 2 months.
- **Reheating:** Not applicable.

Calories	Carbs	Protein	Fat	Fiber	Sodium	Cholesterol	Sugar
110kcal	13g	2g	6g	2g	30mg	0mg	10g

BREAKFAST

CHICKPEA & AVOCADO MASH ON TOASTED GRAIN BREAD

PREP TIME: 10 MINS
COOK TIME: 0 MINS
SERVING: 1

INGREDIENTS

- ½ ripe avocado
- ¼ cup canned chickpeas, mashed
- 1 slice whole grain or sprouted bread
- ½ tsp lemon juice
- Pinch of sea salt and black pepper
- Optional: drizzle of olive oil or sprinkle of crushed red pepper

INSTRUCTIONS

- Toast bread to desired crispness.
- In a small bowl, mash avocado with chickpeas, lemon juice, salt, and pepper.
- Spread the mixture onto toast.
- Top with optional drizzle of olive oil or pepper flakes. Serve immediately.

STORAGE & REHEATING NOTES:

- **Refrigeration:** Best served fresh; mash can be stored up to 1 day in airtight container with lemon juice.
- **Freezing:** Not recommended.
- **Reheating:** Toast bread fresh before assembling.

Calories	Carbs	Protein	Fat	Fiber	Sodium	Cholesterol	Sugar
280kcal	24g	6g	18g	6g	180mg	0mg	1g

CHAPTER 2: LUNCH RECIPES

LUNCH

GRILLED FISH WITH LEMON, GARLIC & HERBS

PREP TIME: 10 MINS
COOK TIME: 12 MINS
SERVING: 2

INGREDIENTS

- 2 fillets of clean fish (e.g., cod, salmon, or tilapia), ~5 oz each
- 1 tbsp olive oil
- 1 garlic clove, minced
- Juice of ½ lemon
- 1 tsp chopped fresh parsley
- ½ tsp dried oregano
- ¼ tsp sea salt
- ¼ tsp black pepper

INSTRUCTIONS

- In a small bowl, mix olive oil, garlic, lemon juice, herbs, salt, and pepper.
- Rub mixture over fish fillets and let marinate for 10 minutes.
- Grill over medium heat for 5–6 minutes per side, or until fish flakes easily.
- Serve hot with additional lemon wedges if desired.

STORAGE & REHEATING NOTES:

- **Refrigeration:** Store in an airtight container up to 2 days.
- **Freezing:** Freeze cooked fish up to 1 month.
- **Reheating:** Reheat gently in oven at 300°F or pan-sear for best texture.

Calories	Carbs	Protein	Fat	Fiber	Sodium	Cholesterol	Sugar
260kcal	2g	26g	15g	0g	220mg	65mg	0g

LUNCH

CUCUMBER & CHICKPEA SALAD WITH OLIVE OIL & DILL

PREP TIME: 10 MINS
COOK TIME: 0 MINS
SERVING: 2

INGREDIENTS

- 1½ cups cooked or canned chickpeas, rinsed
- 1 cucumber, diced
- ¼ cup red onion, finely chopped
- 1 tbsp chopped fresh dill
- 1 tbsp extra virgin olive oil
- 1 tsp lemon juice
- Pinch of sea salt and black pepper

INSTRUCTIONS

- In a bowl, combine chickpeas, cucumber, onion, and dill.
- Drizzle with olive oil and lemon juice.
- Toss gently to combine and season with salt and pepper.
- Chill for 15 minutes or serve immediately.

STORAGE & REHEATING NOTES:

- **Refrigeration:** Store in a sealed container up to 3 days.
- **Freezing:** Not recommended.
- **Reheating:** Serve cold or at room temperature.

Calories	Carbs	Protein	Fat	Fiber	Sodium	Cholesterol	Sugar
220kcal	22g	7g	10g	6g	160mg	0mg	3g

LUNCH

LENTIL & CARROT SOUP WITH CUMIN

PREP TIME: 10 MINS
COOK TIME: 30 MINS
SERVING: 4

INGREDIENTS

- ¾ cup dried brown lentils, rinsed
- 2 carrots, chopped
- ½ onion, diced
- 2 garlic cloves, minced
- 1 tbsp olive oil
- 1 tsp ground cumin
- ¼ tsp ground turmeric
- 4 cups vegetable broth or water
- ½ tsp sea salt
- ¼ tsp black pepper
- Optional: chopped parsley or lemon wedges for serving

INSTRUCTIONS

- In a soup pot, heat olive oil over medium heat. Sauté onion and garlic for 2–3 minutes.
- Add carrots, cumin, turmeric, and stir for 1 minute.
- Stir in lentils, broth, salt, and pepper. Bring to a boil.
- Reduce heat and simmer covered for 25–30 minutes, until lentils and carrots are tender.
- Adjust seasoning. Serve hot with parsley or lemon if desired.

STORAGE & REHEATING NOTES:

- **Refrigeration:** Store in a sealed container up to 4 days.
- **Freezing:** Freeze in individual portions for up to 2 months.
- **Reheating:** Reheat in saucepan or microwave until steaming.

Calories	Carbs	Protein	Fat	Fiber	Sodium	Cholesterol	Sugar
210kcal	28g	10g	6g	8g	380mg	0mg	6g

LUNCH

QUINOA TABOULI WITH PARSLEY, TOMATO & MINT

PREP TIME: 15 MINS
COOK TIME: 15 MINS
SERVING: 3

INGREDIENTS

- ½ cup dry quinoa, rinsed
- 1 cup water
- 1 cup finely chopped fresh parsley
- ¼ cup chopped fresh mint
- 1 tomato, diced
- 2 green onions, chopped
- 2 tbsp olive oil
- 1 tbsp lemon juice
- ¼ tsp sea salt
- ¼ tsp black pepper

INSTRUCTIONS

- In a saucepan, combine quinoa and water. Bring to a boil.
- Reduce heat, cover, and simmer for 12–15 minutes until quinoa is fluffy. Let cool.
- In a bowl, combine parsley, mint, tomato, and green onions.
- Add cooked quinoa, olive oil, lemon juice, salt, and pepper. Toss to combine.
- Chill before serving for best flavor.

STORAGE & REHEATING NOTES:

- **Refrigeration:** Store in the fridge for up to 3 days.
- **Freezing:** Not recommended.
- **Reheating:** Serve chilled or at room temperature.

Calories	Carbs	Protein	Fat	Fiber	Sodium	Cholesterol	Sugar
230kcal	24g	5g	11g	4g	160mg	0mg	2g

LUNCH

CHICKPEA & SPINACH SKILLET WITH OLIVE OIL & GARLIC

PREP TIME: 10 MINS | **COOK TIME:** 10 MINS | **SERVING:** 2

INGREDIENTS

- 1½ cups cooked or canned chickpeas, rinsed
- 2 cups baby spinach, chopped
- 2 tbsp olive oil
- 2 garlic cloves, thinly sliced
- ¼ tsp paprika
- ¼ tsp sea salt
- ⅛ tsp black pepper
- Optional: lemon wedge for serving

INSTRUCTIONS

- Heat olive oil in a skillet over medium heat.
- Add garlic and sauté for 1–2 minutes until fragrant (do not brown).
- Stir in chickpeas, paprika, salt, and pepper. Cook for 3–4 minutes.
- Add spinach and cook for another 2–3 minutes until wilted.
- Serve warm with a squeeze of lemon if desired.

STORAGE & REHEATING NOTES:

- **Refrigeration:** Store in a sealed container for up to 3 days.
- **Freezing:** Freeze up to 1 month.
- **Reheating:** Reheat in a skillet with a splash of water or olive oil.

Calories	Carbs	Protein	Fat	Fiber	Sodium	Cholesterol	Sugar
260kcal	20g	9g	14g	6g	240mg	0mg	3g

LUNCH

ROASTED BEET SALAD WITH GOAT CHEESE & POMEGRANATE

PREP TIME: 10 MINS

COOK TIME: 40 MINS

SERVING: 2

INGREDIENTS

- 2 medium beets, peeled and cubed
- 1 tbsp olive oil
- 1½ cups arugula or mixed greens
- 2 tbsp soft goat cheese
- 2 tbsp pomegranate seeds
- 1 tbsp chopped walnuts
- 1 tsp balsamic vinegar
- Pinch of sea salt and black pepper

INSTRUCTIONS

- Preheat oven to 400ºF (200ºC).
- Toss cubed beets with olive oil, salt, and pepper. Roast on a baking sheet for 35–40 minutes until tender.
- Let beets cool slightly.
- In a bowl, layer greens with roasted beets, goat cheese, pomegranate seeds, and walnuts.
- Drizzle with balsamic vinegar before serving.

STORAGE & REHEATING NOTES:

- **Refrigeration:** Store components separately for up to 3 days.
- **Freezing:** Not recommended.
- **Reheating:** Beets can be gently reheated or served at room temperature.

Calories	Carbs	Protein	Fat	Fiber	Sodium	Cholesterol	Sugar
270kcal	21g	6g	17g	5g	160mg	10mg	9g

LUNCH

BARLEY & FAVA BEAN STEW WITH LEEKS & HERBS

PREP TIME: 10 MINS
COOK TIME: 35 MINS
SERVING: 3

INGREDIENTS

- ½ cup pearl barley
- 1 cup cooked fava beans (or canned, rinsed)
- 1 leek, white and light green parts sliced
- 1 garlic clove, minced
- 2 tbsp olive oil
- ¼ tsp dried thyme
- ¼ tsp sea salt
- 4 cups vegetable broth or water
- Optional: fresh parsley for garnish

INSTRUCTIONS

- Heat olive oil in a pot over medium heat. Sauté garlic and leeks for 2–3 minutes until softened.
- Stir in barley and thyme. Toast for 1 minute.
- Add broth and bring to a boil. Reduce heat and simmer for 25 minutes.
- Stir in fava beans and simmer for another 5–10 minutes until barley is tender.
- Adjust seasoning and garnish with parsley if desired.

STORAGE & REHEATING NOTES:

- **Refrigeration:** Store in an airtight container up to 4 days.
- **Freezing:** Freeze in meal prep portions up to 2 months.
- **Reheating:** Reheat in a saucepan or microwave, adding water as needed.

Calories	Carbs	Protein	Fat	Fiber	Sodium	Cholesterol	Sugar
290kcal	34g	9g	12g	7g	300mg	0mg	3g

LUNCH

STUFFED BELL PEPPERS WITH LENTILS, BROWN RICE & TOMATO

PREP TIME: 15 MINS **COOK TIME:** 30 MINS **SERVING:** 2

INGREDIENTS

- 2 large bell peppers, halved and seeds removed
- ½ cup cooked brown rice
- ½ cup cooked green lentils
- ½ cup diced tomato
- 2 tbsp chopped parsley
- 1 tbsp olive oil
- ½ tsp dried oregano
- ¼ tsp sea salt
- ¼ tsp black pepper

INSTRUCTIONS

- Preheat oven to 375°F (190°C).
- In a bowl, mix rice, lentils, tomato, parsley, olive oil, and seasonings.
- Fill each bell pepper half with the mixture and place in a baking dish.
- Cover loosely with foil and bake for 25–30 minutes until peppers are soft.
- Serve warm.

STORAGE & REHEATING NOTES:

- **Refrigeration:** Store in a sealed container for up to 3 days.
- **Freezing:** Freeze individually wrapped portions up to 1 month.
- **Reheating:** Reheat in oven at 350°F or microwave until heated through.

Calories	Carbs	Protein	Fat	Fiber	Sodium	Cholesterol	Sugar
260kcal	31g	8g	10g	6g	200mg	0mg	5g

LUNCH

SPICED LENTIL WRAPS WITH CUCUMBER YOGURT SAUCE

PREP TIME: 15 MINS
COOK TIME: 20 MINS
SERVING: 2

INGREDIENTS

For the lentils:
- ¾ cup cooked brown or green lentils
- 1 tbsp olive oil
- ¼ tsp ground cumin
- ¼ tsp ground coriander
- ⅛ tsp cayenne (optional)
- ¼ tsp sea salt

For the wraps:
- 2 whole wheat or sprouted grain flatbreads
- ½ cup shredded lettuce or greens
- 1 small tomato, sliced

For the yogurt sauce:
- ¼ cup plain unsweetened yogurt (goat or almond-based)
- ¼ cup finely diced cucumber
- 1 tsp lemon juice
- Pinch of sea salt

INSTRUCTIONS

- In a skillet, heat olive oil and sauté lentils with cumin, coriander, cayenne, and salt for 5–7 minutes.
- Mix yogurt, cucumber, lemon juice, and salt in a small bowl.
- Warm flatbreads, then layer each with greens, tomato, and spiced lentils.
- Drizzle with cucumber yogurt sauce. Roll and serve.

STORAGE & REHEATING NOTES:

- **Refrigeration:** Store fillings and sauce separately for up to 3 days.
- **Freezing:** Lentils only — freeze up to 1 month.
- **Reheating:** Reheat lentils in a skillet or microwave; assemble fresh.

Calories	Carbs	Protein	Fat	Fiber	Sodium	Cholesterol	Sugar
310kcal	32g	10g	14g	7g	280mg	5mg	4g

LUNCH

HERB-GRILLED CHICKEN THIGHS WITH LEMON-TAHINI SAUCE

PREP TIME: 10 MINS   **COOK TIME:** 15 MINS   **SERVING:** 2

INGREDIENTS

For the chicken:
- 2 boneless skinless chicken thighs
- 1 tbsp olive oil
- ½ tsp dried thyme
- ¼ tsp sea salt
- ¼ tsp black pepper

For the sauce:
- 1 tbsp tahini
- 1 tsp lemon juice
- 1 tbsp warm water
- Pinch of sea salt

INSTRUCTIONS

- Rub chicken with olive oil, thyme, salt, and pepper. Let marinate for 10 minutes.
- Grill or pan-sear over medium heat for 6–8 minutes per side until fully cooked.
- Whisk together tahini, lemon juice, warm water, and salt for the sauce.
- Serve chicken drizzled with sauce.

STORAGE & REHEATING NOTES:

- **Refrigeration:** Store in a sealed container for up to 3 days.
- **Freezing:** Freeze cooked chicken up to 1 month.
- **Reheating:** Reheat chicken in a skillet or microwave. Add sauce after reheating.

Calories	Carbs	Protein	Fat	Fiber	Sodium	Cholesterol	Sugar
290kcal	3g	25g	18g	1g	220mg	85mg	1g

LUNCH

FLATBREAD WRAPS WITH HUMMUS, CUCUMBER & GREENS

PREP TIME: 10 MINS | **COOK TIME:** 0 MINS | **SERVING:** 2

INGREDIENTS

- 2 small whole wheat or sprouted flatbreads
- ½ cup hummus (store-bought or homemade)
- ½ cucumber, sliced thin
- 1 small carrot, grated
- 1 cup mixed greens (e.g., arugula, spinach, romaine)
- 1 tsp olive oil
- Optional: dash of lemon juice or fresh herbs (parsley or mint)

INSTRUCTIONS

- Spread ¼ cup hummus on each flatbread.
- Layer with cucumber, grated carrot, and greens.
- Drizzle with olive oil and add optional lemon or herbs.
- Roll up into wraps. Slice in half and serve fresh.

STORAGE & REHEATING NOTES:

- **Refrigeration:** Wrap tightly and refrigerate for up to 1 day (best fresh).
- **Freezing:** Not recommended.
- **Reheating:** Not applicable — serve cold or at room temperature.

Calories	Carbs	Protein	Fat	Fiber	Sodium	Cholesterol	Sugar
270kcal	28g	8g	8g	6g	250mg	0mg	4g

LUNCH: BAKED EGGPLANT WITH TOMATO, ONION & OLIVE OIL

PREP TIME: 15 MINS
COOK TIME: 30 MINS
SERVING: 2

INGREDIENTS

- 1 medium eggplant, sliced into ½-inch rounds
- 1 medium tomato, sliced
- ½ red onion, sliced
- 2 tbsp olive oil
- ½ tsp dried oregano
- ¼ tsp sea salt
- ¼ tsp black pepper
- Optional: fresh basil or parsley for garnish

INSTRUCTIONS

- Preheat oven to 375°F (190°C).
- Layer eggplant, tomato, and onion slices in a baking dish.
- Drizzle with olive oil and season with oregano, salt, and pepper.
- Cover with foil and bake for 20 minutes. Remove foil and bake another 10 minutes until tender and lightly browned.
- Garnish with fresh herbs if desired and serve warm.

STORAGE & REHEATING NOTES:

- **Refrigeration:** Store in a sealed container for up to 3 days.
- **Freezing:** Freeze in single portions up to 1 month.
- **Reheating:** Reheat in oven or skillet until warmed through.

Calories	Carbs	Protein	Fat	Fiber	Sodium	Cholesterol	Sugar
210kcal	18g	3g	14g	5g	200mg	0mg	7g

LUNCH

CAULIFLOWER RICE BOWL WITH OLIVES, CAPERS & CHICKPEAS

PREP TIME: 10 MINS | **COOK TIME:** 10 MINS | **SERVING:** 2

INGREDIENTS

- 2 cups cauliflower rice (fresh or frozen)
- 1 tbsp olive oil
- ½ cup canned chickpeas, rinsed
- ¼ cup chopped cucumber
- 2 tbsp sliced green or black olives
- 1 tsp capers
- ½ tsp dried oregano
- ¼ tsp sea salt
- Optional: lemon wedge for serving

INSTRUCTIONS

- In a skillet, heat olive oil over medium heat. Add cauliflower rice and sauté for 5–7 minutes until soft.
- Stir in chickpeas, oregano, and salt. Cook for 2 more minutes.
- Remove from heat and fold in cucumber, olives, and capers.
- Serve warm or at room temperature with a squeeze of lemon if desired.

STORAGE & REHEATING NOTES:

- **Refrigeration:** Store in a sealed container for up to 3 days.
- **Freezing:** Not recommended.
- **Reheating:** Reheat gently in a skillet or microwave.

Calories	Carbs	Protein	Fat	Fiber	Sodium	Cholesterol	Sugar
230kcal	20g	7g	12g	6g	300mg	0mg	3g

LUNCH

ZUCCHINI FRITTERS WITH HERB YOGURT DIP

PREP TIME: 15 MINS
COOK TIME: 10 MINS
SERVING: 2

INGREDIENTS

For the fritters:
- 1 medium zucchini, grated
- ¼ small onion, finely chopped
- 1 egg
- ¼ cup whole wheat or chickpea flour
- ½ tsp dried dill
- ¼ tsp sea salt
- 2 tbsp olive oil for frying

For the dip:
- ¼ cup plain yogurt (goat or almond-based)
- 1 tsp lemon juice
- ½ tsp chopped fresh mint or parsley
- Pinch of salt

INSTRUCTIONS

- Grate zucchini, then squeeze out excess moisture using a towel.
- In a bowl, combine zucchini, onion, egg, flour, dill, and salt. Mix well.
- Heat olive oil in a skillet over medium heat. Spoon batter to form small fritters and flatten slightly.
- Cook 3–4 minutes per side until golden.
- For the dip, mix yogurt, lemon juice, herbs, and salt.
- Serve fritters with dip on the side.

STORAGE & REHEATING NOTES:

- **Refrigeration:** Store in an airtight container up to 3 days.
- **Freezing:** Freeze cooked fritters up to 1 month.
- **Reheating:** Reheat in skillet or toaster oven until crisp.

Calories	Carbs	Protein	Fat	Fiber	Sodium	Cholesterol	Sugar
260kcal	18g	7g	16g	3g	240mg	55mg	4g

LUNCH

SARDINE SALAD WITH ARUGULA, LEMON & CAPERS

PREP TIME:	COOK TIME:	SERVING:
10 MINS	0 MINS	2

INGREDIENTS

- 1 can sardines in olive oil (about 3.75 oz), drained
- 2 cups arugula or mixed greens
- ½ cup cherry tomatoes, halved
- ¼ small red onion, thinly sliced
- 1 tbsp capers
- 1 tbsp extra virgin olive oil
- 1 tsp lemon juice
- ¼ tsp sea salt
- ¼ tsp black pepper

INSTRUCTIONS

- In a mixing bowl, toss greens, tomatoes, onion, and capers.
- Flake sardines over the salad.
- Drizzle with olive oil and lemon juice.
- Season with salt and pepper. Toss gently and serve immediately.

STORAGE & REHEATING NOTES:

- **Refrigeration:** Best served fresh. Can be refrigerated (undressed) for 1 day.
- **Freezing:** Not recommended.
- **Reheating:** Not applicable.

Calories	Carbs	Protein	Fat	Fiber	Sodium	Cholesterol	Sugar
240kcal	5g	14g	18g	2g	300mg	45mg	2g

CHAPTER 3: DINNER RECIPES

DINNER

ROASTED LAMB WITH ROSEMARY & POMEGRANATE GLAZE

PREP TIME: 15 MINS
COOK TIME: 35 MINS
SERVING: 2

INGREDIENTS

- 2 lamb loin chops (~5 oz each)
- 1 tbsp olive oil
- 1 tsp chopped fresh rosemary (or ½ tsp dried)
- 1 garlic clove, minced
- ¼ tsp sea salt
- ¼ tsp black pepper

For the glaze:
- 2 tbsp 100% pomegranate juice
- 1 tsp raw honey
- ½ tsp apple cider vinegar

INSTRUCTIONS

- Preheat oven to 400ºF (200ºC).
- Rub lamb chops with olive oil, rosemary, garlic, salt, and pepper.
- Sear lamb in a hot skillet for 2 minutes per side. Transfer to oven and roast for 12–15 minutes, or until desired doneness.
- Meanwhile, simmer pomegranate juice, honey, and vinegar in a small saucepan until slightly thickened (5–7 minutes).
- Let lamb rest 5 minutes. Drizzle with glaze before serving.

STORAGE & REHEATING NOTES:

- **Refrigeration:** Store in an airtight container for up to 3 days.
- **Freezing:** Freeze cooked lamb up to 1 month.
- **Reheating:** Reheat in oven at 300ºF until warmed through.

Calories	Carbs	Protein	Fat	Fiber	Sodium	Cholesterol	Sugar
350kcal	6g	28g	22g	1g	180mg	85mg	4g

DINNER

OLIVE OIL-BAKED EGGPLANT WITH TOMATO & BASIL

PREP TIME: 15 MINS
COOK TIME: 30 MINS
SERVING: 2

INGREDIENTS

- 1 large eggplant, cut into ½-inch slices
- 2 tbsp olive oil
- 1 cup cherry tomatoes, halved
- 2 garlic cloves, minced
- ¼ tsp sea salt
- ¼ tsp black pepper
- 1 tbsp chopped fresh basil (or ½ tsp dried)

INSTRUCTIONS

- Preheat oven to 400°F (200°C).
- Arrange eggplant slices on a parchment-lined baking sheet. Brush both sides with olive oil.
- In a bowl, toss tomatoes with garlic, salt, pepper, and basil.
- Spoon tomato mixture over eggplant slices.
- Bake for 25–30 minutes, or until eggplant is tender and golden. Serve warm.

STORAGE & REHEATING NOTES:

- **Refrigeration:** Store in a sealed container up to 3 days.
- **Freezing:** Freeze in single layers up to 1 month.
- **Reheating:** Reheat in oven at 350°F until warmed through.

Calories	Carbs	Protein	Fat	Fiber	Sodium	Cholesterol	Sugar
230kcal	18g	3g	16g	6g	200mg	0mg	7g

DINNER

VEGETABLE STEW WITH LENTILS & BARLEY

PREP TIME: 15 MINS
COOK TIME: 40 MINS
SERVING: 4

INGREDIENTS

- ¾ cup green or brown lentils, rinsed
- ¼ cup pearl barley
- 2 carrots, chopped
- 1 celery stalk, chopped
- 1 zucchini, chopped
- ½ onion, diced
- 2 garlic cloves, minced
- 1 tbsp olive oil
- ½ tsp dried thyme
- ¼ tsp ground cumin
- 5 cups vegetable broth or water
- ½ tsp sea salt
- ¼ tsp black pepper

INSTRUCTIONS

- Heat olive oil in a large pot over medium heat. Sauté onion, garlic, carrot, and celery for 5 minutes.
- Add lentils, barley, zucchini, thyme, cumin, salt, and pepper. Stir to combine.
- Pour in broth and bring to a boil.
- Reduce heat, cover, and simmer for 35–40 minutes until lentils and barley are tender.
- Adjust seasoning and serve warm.

STORAGE & REHEATING NOTES:

- **Refrigeration:** Store in an airtight container for up to 4 days.
- **Freezing:** Freeze in individual portions for up to 2 months.
- **Reheating:** Reheat on stove or microwave until hot; add broth if needed.

Calories	Carbs	Protein	Fat	Fiber	Sodium	Cholesterol	Sugar
280kcal	38g	12g	8g	9g	400mg	0mg	7g

DINNER

BAKED SALMON WITH HERBS & CITRUS

PREP TIME: 10 MINS **COOK TIME:** 15 MINS **SERVING:** 2

INGREDIENTS

- 2 salmon fillets (~5 oz each)
- 1 tbsp olive oil
- Juice of ½ orange
- Juice of ½ lemon
- 1 tsp chopped fresh dill (or ½ tsp dried)
- ¼ tsp sea salt
- ¼ tsp black pepper
- Optional: orange or lemon slices for garnish

INSTRUCTIONS

- Preheat oven to 375°F (190°C).
- Place salmon fillets in a baking dish. Drizzle with olive oil, citrus juices, and season with dill, salt, and pepper.
- Cover loosely with foil and bake for 12–15 minutes, or until salmon flakes easily.
- Garnish with citrus slices if desired and serve warm.

STORAGE & REHEATING NOTES:

- **Refrigeration:** Store in a sealed container for up to 2 days.
- **Freezing:** Freeze cooked salmon up to 1 month.
- **Reheating:** Reheat gently in oven at 300°F or flake into a warm grain bowl.

Calories	Carbs	Protein	Fat	Fiber	Sodium	Cholesterol	Sugar
310kcal	3g	27g	20g	0g	220mg	70mg	2g

DINNER

MEDITERRANEAN LENTIL SHEPHERD'S PIE

PREP TIME: 20 MINS
COOK TIME: 30 MINS
SERVING: 4

INGREDIENTS

For the lentil filling:
- 1 tbsp olive oil
- 1 cup cooked green or brown lentils
- 1 carrot, diced
- ½ onion, diced
- ½ zucchini, chopped
- 1 garlic clove, mince
- 1 tbsp tomato paste
- ½ tsp dried oregano
- ¼ tsp sea salt
- ¼ tsp black pepper

For the topping:
- 2 cups mashed sweet potatoes (about 2 medium)
- 1 tbsp olive oil
- Pinch of salt and cinnamon

INSTRUCTIONS

- Preheat oven to 375°F (190°C).
- In a skillet, heat olive oil. Sauté onion, garlic, carrot, and zucchini for 5 minutes.
- Stir in lentils, tomato paste, oregano, salt, and pepper. Cook for 5 more minutes.
- Spread mixture into a baking dish.
- In a bowl, mix mashed sweet potatoes with olive oil, salt, and cinnamon.
- Spread sweet potato mash over lentil layer.
- Bake for 20–25 minutes until heated through and golden on top.

STORAGE & REHEATING NOTES:

- **Refrigeration:** Store in a sealed container for up to 4 days.
- **Freezing:** Freeze in portions for up to 1 month.
- **Reheating:** Reheat in oven or microwave until warmed through.

Calories	Carbs	Protein	Fat	Fiber	Sodium	Cholesterol	Sugar
320kcal	42g	10g	12g	8g	280mg	0mg	10g

DINNER

HERBED CHICKEN & OLIVE SKILLET WITH DATES

PREP TIME: 15 MINS
COOK TIME: 20 MINS
SERVING: 2

INGREDIENTS

- 2 boneless skinless chicken thighs
- 1 tbsp olive oil
- 2 garlic cloves, minced
- ¼ cup sliced green or black olives
- 2 Medjool dates, chopped
- ½ tsp dried thyme
- ¼ tsp ground cinnamon
- ¼ tsp sea salt
- ¼ tsp black pepper
- Optional: 1 tbsp chopped parsley for garnish

INSTRUCTIONS

- Heat olive oil in a skillet over medium heat. Add chicken and sear 4–5 minutes per side.
- Add garlic, olives, dates, thyme, cinnamon, salt, and pepper. Stir and reduce heat to low.
- Cover and cook for 8–10 more minutes until chicken is cooked through.
- Garnish with fresh parsley if desired and serve warm.

STORAGE & REHEATING NOTES:

- **Refrigeration:** Store in an airtight container for up to 3 days.
- **Freezing:** Freeze cooked chicken in sauce up to 1 month.
- **Reheating:** Reheat gently in a skillet or microwave.

Calories	Carbs	Protein	Fat	Fiber	Sodium	Cholesterol	Sugar
340kcal	9g	26g	22g	2g	340mg	85mg	7g

DINNER

RED LENTIL CURRY WITH SPINACH & GARLIC

PREP TIME: 10 MINS
COOK TIME: 25 MINS
SERVING: 3

INGREDIENTS

- ¾ cup red lentils, rinsed
- 1 tbsp olive oil
- 2 garlic cloves, minced
- 1 small onion, chopped
- 1 tsp ground turmeric
- ½ tsp ground cumin
- ¼ tsp ground coriander
- 3 cups water or vegetable broth
- 2 cups baby spinach
- ½ tsp sea salt
- Optional: lemon wedge for serving

INSTRUCTIONS

- Heat olive oil in a pot. Add onion and garlic; sauté 2–3 minutes.
- Stir in turmeric, cumin, and coriander. Cook 30 seconds until fragrant.
- Add red lentils and broth. Bring to a boil.jjjjj
- Reduce heat and simmer uncovered for 20 minutes, stirring occasionally.
- Add spinach and cook 2 more minutes until wilted.
- Serve warm with lemon if desired.

STORAGE & REHEATING NOTES:

- **Refrigeration:** Store in a sealed container up to 4 days.
- **Freezing:** Freeze in portions up to 2 months.
- **Reheating:** Reheat on stovetop or microwave until hot.

Calories	Carbs	Protein	Fat	Fiber	Sodium	Cholesterol	Sugar
280kcal	30g	14g	10g	8g	300mg	0mg	3g

DINNER

STUFFED GRAPE LEAVES WITH QUINOA & HERBS

PREP TIME: 25 MINS | **COOK TIME:** 30 MINS | **SERVING:** 4

INGREDIENTS

- 12 grape leaves in brine, rinsed and patted dry
- ½ cup cooked quinoa
- ¼ cup chopped parsley
- 2 tbsp chopped fresh mint
- 2 tbsp diced tomato
- 1 tbsp olive oil
- 1 tsp lemon juice
- ¼ tsp sea salt
- ¼ tsp black pepper

INSTRUCTIONS

- Mix quinoa, parsley, mint, tomato, olive oil, lemon juice, salt, and pepper in a bowl.
- Place a grape leaf shiny side down. Add 1 tbsp filling near stem end.
- Fold sides over and roll tightly like a burrito. Repeat with remaining leaves.
- Arrange in a saucepan seam side down. Add ¼ cup water and a drizzle of olive oil.
- Cover and simmer on low heat for 20–30 minutes until leaves are tender.
- Serve warm or chilled.

STORAGE & REHEATING NOTES:

- **Refrigeration:** Store covered for up to 4 days.
- **Freezing:** Freeze in layers with parchment between for up to 1 month.
- **Reheating:** Gently steam or serve cold.

Calories	Carbs	Protein	Fat	Fiber	Sodium	Cholesterol	Sugar
180kcal	22g	4g	9g	3g	300mg	0mg	2g

DINNER

ROASTED ROOT VEGETABLES WITH THYME & GARLIC OIL

PREP TIME: 15 MINS
COOK TIME: 35 MINS
SERVING: 3

INGREDIENTS

- 1 large sweet potato, peeled and cubed
- 2 carrots, peeled and chopped
- 1 parsnip or turnip, chopped
- 1 tbsp olive oil
- 2 garlic cloves, minced
- ½ tsp dried thyme
- ¼ tsp sea salt
- ¼ tsp black pepper
- Optional: fresh parsley for garnish

INSTRUCTIONS

- Preheat oven to 400ºF (200ºC).
- Toss all chopped vegetables with olive oil, garlic, thyme, salt, and pepper.
- Spread evenly on a parchment-lined baking sheet.
- Roast for 30–35 minutes, stirring once, until golden and tender.
- Garnish with parsley if desired. Serve hot.

STORAGE & REHEATING NOTES:

- **Refrigeration:** Store in a sealed container for up to 3 days.
- **Freezing:** Freeze up to 1 month.
- **Reheating:** Reheat in oven or skillet for best texture.

Calories	Carbs	Protein	Fat	Fiber	Sodium	Cholesterol	Sugar
220kcal	28g	3g	11g	5g	200mg	0mg	8g

DINNER

SPAGHETTI SQUASH WITH TOMATO-BASIL SAUCE

PREP TIME: 10 MINS   **COOK TIME:** 40 MINS   **SERVING:** 2

INGREDIENTS

- 1 small spaghetti squash (about 2 lbs)
- 1 tbsp olive oil
- 1½ cups chopped tomatoes (or canned, no salt added)
- 2 garlic cloves, minced
- 1 tsp dried basil
- ¼ tsp sea salt
- ¼ tsp black pepper
- Optional: fresh basil leaves for garnish

INSTRUCTIONS

- Preheat oven to 400°F (200°C). Slice squash in half lengthwise, scoop out seeds, and brush with olive oil.
- Place cut-side down on a baking sheet. Roast for 35–40 minutes until tender.
- Meanwhile, sauté garlic in olive oil for 1 minute. Add tomatoes, basil, salt, and pepper. Simmer 10 minutes.
- Scrape roasted squash with a fork to create strands.
- Top with tomato sauce and garnish with fresh basil.

STORAGE & REHEATING NOTES:

- **Refrigeration:** Store squash and sauce separately for up to 3 days.
- **Freezing:** Freeze strands and sauce separately up to 1 month.
- **Reheating:** Reheat gently in a skillet or microwave.

Calories	Carbs	Protein	Fat	Fiber	Sodium	Cholesterol	Sugar
200kcal	24g	4g	10g	5g	180mg	0mg	9g

DINNER

COD WITH OLIVE TAPENADE & SAUTÉED GREENS

PREP TIME: 10 MINS
COOK TIME: 12 MINS
SERVING: 2

INGREDIENTS

For the cod:
- 2 cod fillets (~5 oz each)
- 1 tbsp olive oil
- ¼ tsp sea salt
- ¼ tsp black pepper

For the tapenade:
- ¼ cup chopped green or black olives
- 1 tsp capers
- ½ tbsp olive oil
- ½ tsp lemon juice

For the greens:
- 2 cups chopped spinach or kale
- 1 tsp olive oil
- 1 garlic clove, sliced

INSTRUCTIONS

- Heat 1 tbsp olive oil in a skillet over medium heat. Season cod with salt and pepper.
- Cook cod for 4–5 minutes per side, or until it flakes easily.
- In a small bowl, mix olives, capers, ½ tbsp olive oil, and lemon juice to make tapenade.
- In another pan, sauté garlic in 1 tsp olive oil for 1 minute. Add greens and cook until wilted.
- Serve cod topped with tapenade, alongside greens.

STORAGE & REHEATING NOTES:

- **Refrigeration:** Store fish and greens separately for up to 2 days.
- **Freezing:** Freeze cooked cod only (not tapenade or greens) for up to 1 month.
- **Reheating:** Reheat gently in skillet or oven; avoid microwave to preserve texture.

Calories	Carbs	Protein	Fat	Fiber	Sodium	Cholesterol	Sugar
300kcal	4g	27g	18g	2g	320mg	65mg	1g

DINNER

WILD RICE & ROASTED CARROT PILAF

PREP TIME: 15 MINS **COOK TIME:** 35 MINS **SERVING:** 2

INGREDIENTS

- ½ cup wild rice, rinsed
- 1¼ cups water or vegetable broth
- 2 carrots, peeled and diced
- 1 tbsp olive oil
- ¼ tsp ground cinnamon
- ¼ tsp sea salt
- 2 tbsp chopped parsley
- Optional: 1 tbsp raisins for a sweet accent

INSTRUCTIONS

- Preheat oven to 400°F (200°C). Toss carrots with olive oil, cinnamon, and a pinch of salt. Roast for 25–30 minutes.
- Meanwhile, cook wild rice: Combine with water or broth in a saucepan. Bring to a boil, reduce to low, cover, and simmer for 30–35 minutes.
- Fluff rice and stir in roasted carrots, parsley, and raisins if using. Serve warm.

STORAGE & REHEATING NOTES:

- **Refrigeration:** Store in a sealed container for up to 4 days.
- **Freezing:** Freeze in portions for up to 1 month.
- **Reheating:** Reheat in a skillet with a splash of water or broth.

Calories	Carbs	Protein	Fat	Fiber	Sodium	Cholesterol	Sugar
270kcal	36g	6g	10g	5g	180mg	0mg	6g

DINNER

VEGETABLE & CHICKPEA TAGINE WITH APRICOTS

PREP TIME: 15 MINS
COOK TIME: 30 MINS
SERVING: 3

INGREDIENTS

- 1 tbsp olive oil
- ½ onion, chopped
- 2 garlic cloves, minced
- 1 carrot, chopped
- 1 zucchini, chopped
- 1½ cups cooked chickpeas
- 4 dried apricots, chopped
- ½ tsp ground cinnamon
- ¼ tsp ground cumin
- ¼ tsp ground ginger
- 2 cups vegetable broth or water
- ¼ tsp sea salt
- Optional: fresh parsley or cilantro for garnish

INSTRUCTIONS

- In a large skillet or pot, heat olive oil over medium. Sauté onion and garlic for 2–3 minutes.
- Add carrot and zucchini. Stir in cinnamon, cumin, and ginger. Cook for 5 minutes.
- Add chickpeas, apricots, broth, and salt.
- Bring to a boil, then reduce heat and simmer uncovered for 20–25 minutes until tender and slightly thickened.
- Garnish with parsley or cilantro if desired.

STORAGE & REHEATING NOTES:

- **Refrigeration:** Store in a sealed container for up to 4 days.
- **Freezing:** Freeze in individual portions for up to 1 month.
- **Reheating:** Reheat in a saucepan or microwave until warm.

Calories	Carbs	Protein	Fat	Fiber	Sodium	Cholesterol	Sugar
290kcal	34g	10g	11g	7g	300mg	0mg	9g

DINNER

CAULIFLOWER & OLIVE GRATIN (NO CHEESE)

PREP TIME: 15 MINS
COOK TIME: 25 MINS
SERVING: 2

INGREDIENTS

- 1 medium head cauliflower, cut into florets
- 2 tbsp olive oil
- ¼ cup chopped green or black olives
- 1 garlic clove, minced
- ½ tsp dried oregano
- ¼ tsp sea salt
- ¼ tsp black pepper
- 2 tbsp almond flour (for topping)

INSTRUCTIONS

- Preheat oven to 375ºF (190ºC).
- Steam cauliflower for 5–7 minutes until just tender. Drain well.
- In a bowl, toss cauliflower with olive oil, olives, garlic, oregano, salt, and pepper.
- Transfer to a small baking dish and sprinkle with almond flour.
- Bake uncovered for 20–25 minutes until lightly browned on top.

STORAGE & REHEATING NOTES:

- **Refrigeration:** Store in an airtight container for up to 3 days.
- **Freezing:** Freeze cooked dish for up to 1 month.
- **Reheating:** Reheat in oven at 350ºF for best texture.

Calories	Carbs	Protein	Fat	Fiber	Sodium	Cholesterol	Sugar
240kcal	14g	5g	18g	6g	300mg	0mg	3g

DINNER

GRILLED EGGPLANT & TOMATO STACKS WITH GARLIC OIL

PREP TIME: 15 MINS
COOK TIME: 20 MINS
SERVING: 2

INGREDIENTS

- 1 medium eggplant, sliced into ½-inch rounds
- 2 medium tomatoes, sliced
- 2 tbsp olive oil
- 1 garlic clove, minced
- ½ tsp dried oregano
- ¼ tsp sea salt
- ¼ tsp black pepper
- Optional: fresh basil for garnish

INSTRUCTIONS

- Brush eggplant slices with 1 tbsp olive oil and sprinkle with salt, pepper, and oregano.
- Grill on a grill pan or outdoor grill for 4–5 minutes per side until tender.
- Meanwhile, mix remaining olive oil with minced garlic.
- Stack grilled eggplant and tomato slices in alternating layers (2–3 per stack).
- Drizzle with garlic oil and garnish with basil if desired. Serve warm.

STORAGE & REHEATING NOTES:

- **Refrigeration:** Store stacks in a sealed container for up to 2 days.
- **Freezing:** Not recommended.
- **Reheating:** Warm gently in oven or skillet.

Calories	Carbs	Protein	Fat	Fiber	Sodium	Cholesterol	Sugar
280kcal	34g	21g	8g	5g	60mg	5mg	20g

CHAPTER 1:
DRINKS & HEALING TONICS

DRINKS & HEALING TONICS

POMEGRANATE & HONEY TONIC

PREP TIME: 5 MINS
COOK TIME: 0 MINS
SERVING: 1

INGREDIENTS

- ½ cup pure pomegranate juice (unsweetened)
- ½ cup filtered water
- 1 tsp raw honey
- 1 tsp apple cider vinegar (with the mother)
- Optional: pinch of sea salt

INSTRUCTIONS

- In a glass, mix pomegranate juice and water.
- Stir in honey and apple cider vinegar until dissolved.
- Add a pinch of sea salt if desired. Serve at room temperature or over ice.

STORAGE & REHEATING NOTES:

- **Refrigeration:** Best made fresh, but can be stored for up to 1 day.
- **Freezing:** Not recommended.
- **Reheating:** Not applicable (served cold or room temp).

Calories	Carbs	Protein	Fat	Fiber	Sodium	Cholesterol	Sugar
80kcal	19g	0g	0g	0g	30mg	0mg	17g

DRINKS & HEALING TONICS

LEMON & OLIVE OIL DETOX DRINK

PREP TIME: 5 MINS

COOK TIME: 0 MINS

SERVING: 1

INGREDIENTS

- Juice of ½ lemon (about 1 tbsp)
- 1 tbsp extra virgin olive oil
- ¾ cup warm filtered water
- Pinch of cayenne (optional)

INSTRUCTIONS

- In a small glass, mix lemon juice with olive oil.
- Add warm water and stir until well blended.
- Sprinkle in cayenne if using and drink slowly on an empty stomach.

STORAGE & REHEATING NOTES:

- **Refrigeration:** Not recommended—make fresh.
- **Freezing:** Not recommended.
- **Reheating:** If it cools, rewarm water gently (not boiling).

Calories	Carbs	Protein	Fat	Fiber	Sodium	Cholesterol	Sugar
130kcal	1g	0g	14g	0g	5mg	0mg	0g

DRINKS & HEALING TONICS

CINNAMON & CLOVE HERBAL TEA

PREP TIME: 5 MINS
COOK TIME: 10 MINS
SERVING: 2

INGREDIENTS

- 2 cups filtered water
- 1 cinnamon stick
- 4 whole cloves
- Optional: ½ tsp raw honey (added after steeping)

INSTRUCTIONS

- In a small saucepan, bring water to a gentle boil.
- Add cinnamon stick and cloves. Reduce heat and simmer for 10 minutes.
- Strain and pour into mugs. Add honey if desired. Serve warm.

STORAGE & REHEATING NOTES:

- **Refrigeration:** Store in the fridge up to 2 days.
- **Freezing:** Not recommended.
- **Reheating:** Reheat gently on the stovetop until warm.

Calories	Carbs	Protein	Fat	Fiber	Sodium	Cholesterol	Sugar
10kcal	3g	0g	0g	0g	0mg	0mg	2g

DRINKS & HEALING TONICS

FIG & DATE SMOOTHIE

PREP TIME: 5 MINS **COOK TIME:** 0 MINS **SERVING:** 1

INGREDIENTS

- 2 dried figs, stems removed
- 2 Medjool dates, pitted
- 1 cup unsweetened almond milk or water
- ¼ tsp cinnamon
- 1 tbsp chia seeds (optional)

INSTRUCTIONS

- Soak figs and dates in warm water for 5 minutes if very dry.
- Add all ingredients to a blender and blend until smooth.
- Pour into a glass and enjoy chilled or room temperature.

STORAGE & REHEATING NOTES:

- **Refrigeration:** Best served immediately, but can refrigerate up to 1 day.
- **Freezing:** Not recommended.
- **Reheating:** Not applicable (serve cold or room temp).

Calories	Carbs	Protein	Fat	Fiber	Sodium	Cholesterol	Sugar
180kcal	36g	2g	4g	5g	90mg	0mg	29g

DRINKS & HEALING TONICS

CINNAMON & CLOVE HERBAL TEA

PREP TIME: 5 MINS
COOK TIME: 10 MINS
SERVING: 2

INGREDIENTS

- 2 cups filtered water
- 1 cinnamon stick
- 4 whole cloves
- Optional: ½ tsp raw honey (added after steeping)

INSTRUCTIONS

- In a small saucepan, bring water to a gentle boil.
- Add cinnamon stick and cloves. Reduce heat and simmer for 10 minutes.
- Strain and pour into mugs. Add honey if desired. Serve warm.

STORAGE & REHEATING NOTES:

- **Refrigeration:** Store in the fridge up to 2 days.
- **Freezing:** Not recommended.
- **Reheating:** Reheat gently on the stovetop until warm.

Calories	Carbs	Protein	Fat	Fiber	Sodium	Cholesterol	Sugar
10kcal	0g	0g	0g	0g	0mg	0mg	2g

DRINKS & HEALING TONICS

FIG & DATE SMOOTHIE

PREP TIME: 5 MINS | **COOK TIME:** 0 MINS | **SERVING:** 1

INGREDIENTS

- 2 dried figs, stems removed
- 2 Medjool dates, pitted
- 1 cup unsweetened almond milk or water
- ¼ tsp cinnamon
- 1 tbsp chia seeds (optional)

INSTRUCTIONS

- Soak figs and dates in warm water for 5 minutes if very dry.
- Add all ingredients to a blender and blend until smooth.
- Pour into a glass and enjoy chilled or room temperature.

STORAGE & REHEATING NOTES:

- **Refrigeration:** Best served immediately, but can refrigerate up to 1 day.
- **Freezing:** Not recommended.
- **Reheating:** Not applicable (serve cold or room temp).

Calories	Carbs	Protein	Fat	Fiber	Sodium	Cholesterol	Sugar
180kcal	36g	2g	4g	5g	90mg	0mg	29g

DRINKS & HEALING TONICS

WARM APPLE CIDER VINEGAR TONIC

PREP TIME: 5 MINS | **COOK TIME:** 0 MINS | **SERVING:** 1

INGREDIENTS

- 1 cup warm filtered water
- 1 tbsp raw apple cider vinegar (with the mother)
- 1 tsp raw honey (optional)
- Dash of cinnamon
- Optional: slice of fresh ginger

INSTRUCTIONS

- Warm the water (not boiling).
- Stir in apple cider vinegar, honey, cinnamon, and ginger if using.
- Mix well and sip slowly on an empty stomach.

STORAGE & REHEATING NOTES:

- **Refrigeration:** Not recommended.
- **Freezing:** Not recommended.
- **Reheating:** Best made fresh and served warm.

Calories	Carbs	Protein	Fat	Fiber	Sodium	Cholesterol	Sugar
25kcal	6g	0g	0g	0g	5mg	0mg	5g

DRINKS & HEALING TONICS

CARROT & ORANGE JUICE WITH GINGER

PREP TIME: 10 MINS   **COOK TIME:** 0 MINS   **SERVING:** 1

INGREDIENTS

- 2 large carrots, peeled and chopped
- 1 large orange, peeled
- ½ inch fresh ginger, peeled
- ½ cup cold filtered water

INSTRUCTIONS

- Add carrots, orange, ginger, and water to a blender.
- Bend until smooth.
- Strain through a fine mesh sieve or cheesecloth if desired.
- Serve chilled.

STORAGE & REHEATING NOTES:

- **Refrigeration:** Store in an airtight container for up to 1 day.
- **Freezing:** Not recommended.
- **Reheating:** Not applicable.

Calories	Carbs	Protein	Fat	Fiber	Sodium	Cholesterol	Sugar
90kcal	20g	1g	0g	3g	60mg	0mg	14g

WATERMELON & BASIL HYDRATION JUICE

DRINKS & HEALING TONICS

PREP TIME: 10 MINS
COOK TIME: 0 MINS
SERVING: 2

INGREDIENTS

- 2 cups seedless watermelon, cubed
- ½ cup cold filtered water
- 2–3 fresh basil leaves
- Juice of ½ lime (optional)

INSTRUCTIONS

- Add watermelon and water to a blender.
- Blend until smooth. Add basil and pulse 2–3 times.
- Strain if desired, then serve chilled with lime juice if using.

STORAGE & REHEATING NOTES:

- **Refrigeration:** Store for up to 1 day. Stir before serving.
- **Freezing:** Not recommended.
- **Reheating:** Not applicable.

Calories	Carbs	Protein	Fat	Fiber	Sodium	Cholesterol	Sugar
50kcal	13g	1g	0g	1g	5mg	0mg	10g

DRINKS & HEALING TONICS

DATES & ALMOND MILK SPICED LATTE (CAFFEINE-FREE)

PREP TIME: 5 MINS **COOK TIME:** 5 MINS **SERVING:** 1

INGREDIENTS

- 1 cup unsweetened almond milk
- 2 Medjool dates, pitted
- ¼ tsp cinnamon
- ¼ tsp vanilla extract
- Pinch of nutmeg

INSTRUCTIONS

- Blend almond milk and dates until smooth.
- Pour into a saucepan and add cinnamon, vanilla, and nutmeg.
- Warm over low heat, stirring gently. Serve warm.

STORAGE & REHEATING NOTES:

- **Refrigeration:** Store in fridge up to 1 day.
- **Freezing:** Not recommended.
- **Reheating:** Reheat gently over low heat.

Calories	Carbs	Protein	Fat	Fiber	Sodium	Cholesterol	Sugar
1120kcal	22g	2g	3g	2g	150mg	0mg	18g

CONCLUSION

The Biblio Diet is more than a collection of recipes. It is a return to the roots of nourishment, the rhythms of creation, and the wisdom found in Scripture. In a world full of conflicting advice and complicated rules, this approach invites you to slow down, simplify, and align your daily habits with timeless truth.

You do not need to count every calorie or follow a rigid system to feel better. What you need is structure, intention, and a reminder that your body was designed to heal when supported with real food, rest, and rhythm. The meals in this book are meant to help you do just that.

Whether you are just beginning your health journey or renewing your commitment to faith-filled living, this cookbook can be your starting point. Let each meal be a quiet act of restoration. Let every fast be a moment of reflection. Let food become a way to honor your body and glorify God.

As you step into this new rhythm of eating and living, may you experience more energy, peace, clarity, and joy. You were never meant to walk this journey alone. With every meal, you have an opportunity to reconnect—with your health, your purpose, and your faith.

Your table can be a place of healing. Start today.

"He fills the hungry with good things."

Luke 1:53 (NIV)

30 DAYS MEAL PLAN

WEEK 1

Day	Breakfast	Lunch	Dinner	Drinks
1	Honey & Fig Yogurt Bowl Page 7	Grilled Fish with Lemon, Garlic & Herbs Page 23	Roasted Lamb with Rosemary & Pomegranate Glaze Page 39	Pomegranate & Honey Tonic Page 55
2	Barley Porridge with Dates & Almond Milk Page 8	Cucumber & Chickpea Salad with Olive Oil & Dill Page 24	Olive Oil-Baked Eggplant with Tomato & Basil Page 40	Lemon & Olive Oil Detox Drink Page 56
3	Olive Oil & Herb Flatbread with Roasted Vegetables Page 9	Lentil & Carrot Soup with Cumin Page 25	Vegetable Stew with Lentils & Barley Page 41	Cinnamon & Clove Herbal Tea Page 57
4	Lentil & Egg Scramble with Za'atar Page 10	Quinoa Tabouli with Parsley, Tomato & Mint Page 26	Baked Salmon with Herbs & Citrus Page 42	Fig & Date Smoothie Page 58
5	Roasted Sweet Potato Hash with Red Onions & Thyme Page 11	Chickpea & Spinach Skillet with Olive Oil & Garlic Page 27	Mediterranean Lentil Shepherd's Pie Page 43	Warm Apple Cider Vinegar Tonic Page 59
6	Shepherd's Breakfast Bowl Page 12	Roasted Beet Salad with Goat Cheese & Pomegranate Page 28	Herbed Chicken & Olive Skillet with Dates Page 44	Carrot & Orange Juice with Ginger Page 60
7	Apple & Raisin Millet Porridge with Cinnamon Page 13	Barley & Fava Bean Stew with Leeks & Herbs Page 29	Red Lentil Curry with Spinach & Garlic Page 45	Watermelon & Basil Hydration Juice Page 61

30 DAYS MEAL PLAN

WEEK 2

Day	Breakfast	Lunch	Dinner	Drinks
8	Baked Pears with Walnuts & Raw Honey Page 14	Stuffed Bell Peppers with Lentils, Brown Rice & Tomato Page 30	Stuffed Grape Leaves with Quinoa & Herbs Page 46	Dates & Almond Milk Spiced Latte Page 62
9	Goat Cheese & Tomato Omelet with Herbs Page 15	Spiced Lentil Wraps with Cucumber Yogurt Sauce Page 31	Roasted Root Vegetables with Thyme & Garlic Oil Page 47	Pomegranate & Honey Tonic Page 63
10	Ezekiel Bread Toast with Olive Tapenade & Boiled Egg Page 16	Herb-Grilled Chicken Thighs with Lemon-Tahini Sauce Page 32	Spaghetti Squash with Tomato-Basil Sauce Page 48	Watermelon & Basil Hydration Juice Page 61
11	Carrot-Date Muffins with Almond Flour Page 17	Flatbread Wraps with Hummus, Cucumber & Greens Page 33	Cod with Olive Tapenade & Sautéed Greens Page 49	Cinnamon & Clove Herbal Tea Page 57
12	Grape & Quinoa Breakfast Salad with Mint & Olive Oil Page 18	Baked Eggplant with Tomato, Onion & Olive Oil Page 34	Wild Rice & Roasted Carrot Pilaf Page 50	Pomegranate & Honey Tonic Page 55
13	Mashed Fava Beans with Olive Oil & Flatbread Page 19	Cauliflower Rice Bowl with Olives, Capers & Chickpeas Page 35	Vegetable & Chickpea Tagine with Apricots Page 51	Lemon & Olive Oil Detox Drink Page 56
14	Date & Almond Energy Bites with Ground Flax Page 20	Zucchini Fritters with Herb Yogurt Dip Page 36	Cauliflower & Olive Gratin (No Cheese) Page 52	Warm Apple Cider Vinegar Tonic Page 59

30 DAYS MEAL PLAN

WEEK 3

Day	Breakfast	Lunch	Dinner	Drinks
15	Chickpea & Avocado Mash on Toasted Grain Bread Page 21	Sardine Salad with Arugula, Lemon & Capers Page 37	Grilled Eggplant & Tomato Stacks with Garlic Oil Page 53	Warm Apple Cider Vinegar Tonic Page 59
16	Mashed Fava Beans with Olive Oil & Flatbread Page 19	Lentil & Carrot Soup with Cumin Page 25	Wild Rice & Roasted Carrot Pilaf Page 50	Pomegranate & Honey Tonic Page 63
17	Apple & Raisin Millet Porridge with Cinnamon Page 13	Quinoa Tabouli with Parsley, Tomato & Mint Page 26	Red Lentil Curry with Spinach & Garlic Page 45	Lemon & Olive Oil Detox Drink Page 56
18	Date & Almond Energy Bites with Ground Flax Page 20	Roasted Beet Salad with Goat Cheese & Pomegranate Page 28	Herbed Chicken & Olive Skillet with Dates Page 44	Fig & Date Smoothie Page 58
19	Honey & Fig Yogurt Bowl Page 7	Flatbread Wraps with Hummus, Cucumber & Greens Page 33	Mediterranean Lentil Shepherd's Pie Page 43	Dates & Almond Milk Spiced Latte Page 62
20	Lentil & Egg Scramble with Za'atar Page 10	Zucchini Fritters with Herb Yogurt Dip Page 36	Vegetable Stew with Lentils & Barley Page 41	Carrot & Orange Juice with Ginger Page 60
21	Goat Cheese & Tomato Omelet with Herbs Page 15	Stuffed Bell Peppers with Lentils, Brown Rice & Tomato Page 30	Roasted Root Vegetables with Thyme & Garlic Oil Page 47	Watermelon & Basil Hydration Juice Page 61

30 DAYS MEAL PLAN

WEEK 4

Day	Breakfast	Lunch	Dinner	Drinks
22	Honey & Fig Yogurt Bowl Page 7	Grilled Fish with Lemon, Garlic & Herbs Page 23	Olive Oil-Baked Eggplant with Tomato & Basil Page 40	Warm Apple Cider Vinegar Tonic Page 59
24	Shepherd's Breakfast Bowl Page 12	Barley & Fava Bean Stew with Leeks & Herbs Page 29	Baked Salmon with Herbs & Citrus Page 42	Dates & Almond Milk Spiced Latte Page 62
25	Carrot-Date Muffins with Almond Flour Page 17	Lentil & Carrot Soup with Cumin Page 25	Cod with Olive Tapenade & Sautéed Greens Page 49	Watermelon & Basil Hydration Juice Page 61
26	Date & Almond Energy Bites with Ground Flax Page 20	Spiced Lentil Wraps with Cucumber Yogurt Sauce Page 31	Wild Rice & Roasted Carrot Pilaf Page 50	Carrot & Orange Juice with Ginger Page 60
27	Apple & Raisin Millet Porridge with Cinnamon Page 13	Zucchini Fritters with Herb Yogurt Dip Page 36	Grilled Eggplant & Tomato Stacks with Garlic Oil Page 53	Fig & Date Smoothie Page 58
28	Barley Porridge with Dates & Almond Milk Page 8	Cucumber & Chickpea Salad with Olive Oil & Dill Page 24	Cauliflower & Olive Gratin Page 52	Cinnamon & Clove Herbal Tea Page 57
29	Honey & Fig Yogurt Bowl Page 7	Barley & Fava Bean Stew with Leeks & Herbs Page 29	Herbed Chicken & Olive Skillet with Dates Page 44	Fig & Date Smoothie Page 58

WEEK 1 SHOPPING LIST

(General list based on meals from Week 1 of the 30-Day Meal Plan. Quantities are approximate and can be adjusted based on household size and serving needs.)

PROTEINS – DAIRY-FREE
- ☐ Chicken breast
- ☐ Salmon
- ☐ Tuna
- ☐ Shrimp
- ☐ Tofu
- ☐ Tempeh
- ☐ Chickpeas
- ☐ Black Beans

PROTEINS – DAIRY
- ☐ Greek yogurt
- ☐ Cottage cheese
- ☐ Mozzarella
- ☐ Feta cheese
- ☐ Parmesan cheese
- ☐ Ricotta cheese
- ☐ Swiss cheese

VEGETABLES
- ☐ Spinach
- ☐ Kale
- ☐ Cucumbers
- ☐ Asparagus
- ☐ Bell pepper
- ☐ Green beans
- ☐ Broccoli florets
- ☐ Cauliflower
- ☐ Mushrooms
- ☐ Parsley
- ☐ Lemons
- ☐ Garlic

FRUITS
- ☐ Blueberries
- ☐ Apples
- ☐ Mango
- ☐ Kiwi

NUTS & SEEDS
- ☐ Almonds
- ☐ Walnuts
- ☐ Cashews
- ☐ Pecans
- ☐ Pistachios
- ☐ Flaxseeds
- ☐ Hemp seeds

OTHER ESSENTIALS (DAIRY-FREE)
- ☐ Olive oil
- ☐ Coconut oil
- ☐ Coconut yogurt
- ☐ Nutritional yeast
- ☐ Tahini
- ☐ Hummus
- ☐ Apple cider vinegar
- ☐ Honey
- ☐ Coconut milk

WEEK 2 SHOPPING LIST

(General list based on meals from Week 2 of the 30-Day Meal Plan. Quantities are approximate and can be adjusted based on household size and serving needs.)

PROTEINS – DAIRY-FREE
☐ Cod
☐ Tilapia
☐ Sardines
☐ Ground turkey
☐ Egg whites
☐ Edamame
☐ Kidney beans
☐ Quinoa

PROTEINS – DAIRY
☐ Brie
☐ Gouda
☐ Cream cheese
☐ Yogurt (plain)
☐ Blue cheese
☐ Whey protein
☐ Swiss cheese

VEGETABLES
☐ Romaine
☐ Arugula
☐ Swiss chard
☐ Beets
☐ Brussels sprouts
☐ Green beans
☐ Cabbage
☐ Cauliflower
☐ Eggplant
☐ Parsley
☐ Celery
☐ Radishes

FRUITS
☐ Pears
☐ Peaches
☐ Plum
☐ Cherries

NUTS & SEEDS
☐ Hazelnuts
☐ Brazil nuts
☐ Macadamia nuts
☐ Pine nuts
☐ Sesame seeds
☐ Poppy seeds
☐ Nigella seeds

OTHER ESSENTIALS (DAIRY-FREE)
☐ Avocado oil
☐ Sesame oil
☐ Soy milk
☐ Cashew milk
☐ Coconut cream
☐ Miso paste
☐ Apple cider vinegar
☐ Tamari
☐ Tomato paste

WEEK 3 SHOPPING LIST

(General list based on meals from Week 3 of the 30-Day Meal Plan. Quantities are approximate and can be adjusted based on household size and serving needs.)

PROTEINS – DAIRY-FREE
☐ Haddock
☐ Mahi mahi
☐ Anchovies
☐ Scallops
☐ Crabs
☐ Lobsters
☐ Duck breast
☐ Bison

PROTEINS – DAIRY
☐ Camembert
☐ Romano
☐ Cream cheese
☐ Yogurt (plain)
☐ Mascarpone
☐ Whey protein
☐ Goat cheese

VEGETABLES
☐ Lettuce
☐ Collard Greens
☐ Turnips
☐ Parsnips
☐ Artichokes
☐ Okra
☐ Leeks
☐ Onions
☐ Eggplant
☐ Parsley
☐ Cilantro
☐ Radishes

FRUITS
☐ Clementines
☐ Apricots
☐ Passionfruits
☐ Figs

NUTS & SEEDS
☐ Mixed nuts
☐ Almond butter
☐ Sunflower seed
☐ Chestnuts
☐ Sesame seeds
☐ Poppy seeds
☐ Flax meal

OTHER ESSENTIALS (DAIRY-FREE)
☐ Walnut oil
☐ Rice milk
☐ Vegan butter
☐ Cashew milk
☐ Coconut cream
☐ Coconut aminos
☐ Apple cider vinegar
☐ Salsa
☐ Dark chocolate

WEEK 4 SHOPPING LIST

(General list based on meals from Week 4 of the 30-Day Meal Plan. Quantities are approximate and can be adjusted based on household size and serving needs.)

PROTEINS – DAIRY-FREE
☐ Swordfish
☐ Halibut
☐ Anchovies
☐ Clams
☐ Eggs
☐ Lobsters
☐ Duck breast
☐ Red lentils

PROTEINS – DAIRY
☐ Yogurt, unsweetened
☐ Sour cream
☐ Cream cheese
☐ Yogurt (plain)
☐ Mozzarella Cheese
☐ Whey protein
☐ Goat cheese

VEGETABLES
☐ Mustard green
☐ Collard Greens
☐ Peas
☐ Parsnips
☐ Broccoli
☐ Okra
☐ Leeks
☐ Ginger
☐ Eggplant
☐ Parsley
☐ Cilantro
☐ Garlic

FRUITS
☐ Cranberries
☐ Apple
☐ Jackfruit
☐ Pineapple

NUTS & SEEDS
☐ Caraway seeds
☐ Pecans
☐ Pistachios
☐ Chestnuts
☐ Walnuts
☐ Poppy seeds
☐ Watermelon seeds

OTHER ESSENTIALS (DAIRY-FREE)
☐ Grapeseed oil
☐ Sesame paste
☐ Vegan butter
☐ Coconut sugar
☐ Coconut cream
☐ Coconut butter
☐ Vinegar
☐ Dijon mustard
☐ Sriracha

INDEX

A
Apple & Raisin Millet Porridge with Cinnamon, 13

B
Baked Eggplant with Tomato, Onion & Olive Oil, 34
Baked Pears with Walnuts & Raw Honey, 14
Baked Salmon with Herbs & Citrus, 42
Barley & Fava Bean Stew with Leeks & Herbs, 29
Barley Porridge with Dates & Almond Milk, 8

C
Carrot & Orange Juice with Ginger, 62
Carrot-Date Muffins with Almond Flour, 17
Cauliflower & Olive Gratin (No Cheese), 52
Cauliflower Rice Bowl with Olives, Capers & Chickpeas, 35
Chickpea & Avocado Mash on Toasted Grain Bread, 21
Chickpea & Spinach Skillet with Olive Oil & Garlic, 27
Cinnamon & Clove Herbal Tea, 57
Cinnamon & Clove Herbal Tea, 59
Cod with Olive Tapenade & Sautéed Greens, 49
Cucumber & Chickpea Salad with Olive Oil & Dill, 24

D
Date & Almond Energy Bites with Ground Flax, 20
Dates & Almond Milk Spiced Latte, 64

E
Ezekiel Bread Toast with Olive Tapenade & Boiled Egg, 16

F
Fig & Date Smoothie, 60
Fig & Date Smoothie, 58
Flatbread Wraps with Hummus, Cucumber & Greens, 33

G
Goat Cheese & Tomato Omelet with Herbs, 15
Grape & Quinoa Breakfast Salad with Mint & Olive Oil, 18
Grilled Eggplant & Tomato Stacks with Garlic Oil, 53
Grilled Fish with Lemon, Garlic & Herbs, 23

H
Herbed Chicken & Olive Skillet with Dates, 44
Herb-Grilled Chicken Thighs with Lemon-Tahini Sauce, 32
Honey & Fig Yogurt Bowl, 7

L
Lemon & Olive Oil Detox Drink, 56
Lentil & Carrot Soup with Cumin, 25
Lentil & Egg Scramble with Za'atar, 10

M
Mashed Fava Beans with Olive Oil & Flatbread, 19
Mediterranean Lentil Shepherd's Pie, 43

O

Olive Oil & Herb Flatbread with Roasted Vegetables, 9

Olive Oil-Baked Eggplant with Tomato & Basil, 40

P

Pomegranate & Honey Tonic, 55

Q

Quinoa Tabouli with Parsley, Tomato & Mint, 26

R

Red Lentil Curry with Spinach & Garlic, 45

Roasted Beet Salad with Goat Cheese & Pomegranate, 28

Roasted Lamb with Rosemary & Pomegranate Glaze, 39

Roasted Root Vegetables with Thyme & Garlic Oil, 47

Roasted Sweet Potato Hash with Red Onions & Thyme, 11

S

Sardine Salad with Arugula, Lemon & Capers, 37

Shepherd's Breakfast Bowl with Chickpeas & Cucumber Yogurt, 12

Spaghetti Squash with Tomato-Basil Sauce, 48

Spiced Lentil Wraps with Cucumber Yogurt Sauce, 31

Stuffed Bell Peppers with Lentils, Brown Rice & Tomato, 30

Stuffed Grape Leaves with Quinoa & Herbs, 46

V

Vegetable & Chickpea Tagine with Apricots, 51

Vegetable Stew with Lentils & Barley, 41

W

Warm Apple Cider Vinegar Tonic, 61

Watermelon & Basil Hydration Juice, 63

Wild Rice & Roasted Carrot Pilaf, 50

Z

Zucchini Fritters with Herb Yogurt Dip, 36

Made in the USA
Columbia, SC
09 October 2025